The Introduction of AI
For Class VIII Students

by

Er. Ashish Tripathi

Double 9 BOOKS

ABOUT THE AUTHOR

The Author belongs to Varanasi Distt Uttar Pradesh India and has been simple personality and working in education sectors as IT Professionals. He did Bachelor Degree in Physics, Computer Science, and also Mathematics and in Post graduation he completed MCA (Master of Computer Application) and M.Tech (Master of Technology in Information Technology). He worked four years as Assistant Professor in Centre for Management Technology Gr. Noida and also Guest Faculty in various engineering colleges and past few years currently he works in CBSE Board affiliated School education systems as IT/ Computer Science faculty in such a branded schools in Varanasi Distt like Raj English School Varanasi, Dalimss Sunbeam Group of Institutions Varanasi UP, & PGT CS (contract) JNV Gov of India. Currently worked as contract based Computer Science Faculty in Navodaya Vidyalaya Samiti. He has been achieved more than 35 certificates from Microsoft Education and Community. The author have been able to utilize the problem solving skills to achieve Top grades in challenging course like Numerical methods, Artificial Intelligence, Software engineering, Client/Server Computing and Networking. The Author prays to "Maa Aadishakti" that this journey of knowledge continues in his life. I express my specially thanks to Mr.Ajit Kumar Singh (Principal, NVS, Gov Of India) and Mr. Arvind Pratap Singh (Director, Sunbeam School Cholapur Varanasi UP) who have guided every time for skills education to students and encourage me their moral support for this project and also specially thanks to Mr. Rana Devanand Singh (PGT Hindi, NVS Gov of India) for their constant encouragement. I also thank to Mr. Vikash Srivastava (PGT Maths, NVS Gov of India), Mr. Arun Kumar Mishra (PGT Teacher, NVS, Gov of India) and Mrs. Neera Singh (PET, NVS Gov of India) support us suggest every moments. I thankfully to my friend Mr. Saurabh Upadhyay (MCA, B.ed, Teacher Gov OF UP),Mr. Rajesh Sukla Sir (PGT Biology JNV Champawat Gov of India) and Mr. Vivek Agrawal (PGT Commerce, EMRS Gov. of India) for their direct and indirect moral support.

CONTENTS

Syllabus:

According to CBSE Board new AI Skilled based subject develop a syllabus to class VIII students. Students will be able to learn some highlighted points:

- Identify and appreciate Artificial Intelligence and describe its applications in daily life.

- Relate, apply and reflect on the Human-Machine Interactions.

- Identify and interact with the three domains of AI: Data, Computer Vision and Natural Language Processing.

- Undergo assessment for analyzing their progress towards acquired AI-Readiness skills.

- Imagine, examine and reflect on the skills required for the futuristic opportunities.

- Unleash their imagination towards smart homes and build an interactive story around it.

- Understand the impact of Artificial Intelligence on Sustainable Development Goals to develop responsible citizenship.

- Research and develop awareness of skills required for jobs of the future.

- Describe the potential ethical considerations of AI.

- Awareness about AI bias and AI access.

- Develop effective communication and collaborative work skills.

AI syllabus categories in five units and each unit have creativity and some practical modules to learn their inner strengths.

Unit	Activity/Session	Learning Outcome
1- EXCITE	Session: Introduction to AI and setting up the context of the curriculum	To identify and appreciate Artificial Intelligence and describe its applications in daily life.
	Ice Breaker Activity: Dream Smart Home idea	To relate, apply and reflect on the Human-Machine Interactions.
	Learners to design a rough layout of floor plan of their dream smart home.	To identify and interact with the three domains of AI: Data, Computer Vision and Natural Language Processing.
	Recommended Activity: The AI Game	To undergo an assessment for analyzing progress towards acquired AI-Readiness skills.
	Learners to participate in three games based on different AI domains.	To imagine, examine and reflect on the skills required for the futuristic opportunities.
	• Game 1: Rock, Paper and Scissors (based on data)	
	• Game 2: Mystery Animal (based on Natural Language Processing - NLP)	
	• Game 3: Emoji Scavenger Hunt (based on Computer Vision - CV)	
	Recommended Activity: AI Quiz (Paper Pen/Online Quiz)	
	Recommended Activity: To write a letter	
	Writing a Letter to one's future self.	
	Learners to write a letter to self-keeping the future in context. They will describe what they have learnt so far or what they would like to learn someday	
	Video Session: To watch a video	
	Introducing the concept of Smart Cities, Smart Schools and Smart Homes	

2- RELATE	Video Session: To watch a video Introducing the concept of Smart Cities, Smart Schools and Smart Homes	Learners to relate to application of Artificial Intelligence in their daily lives.
	Recommended Activity:	To unleash their imagination towards smart homes and build an interactive story around it.
	To write an Interactive Story Learners to draw a floor plan of a Home/School/City and write an interactive story around it using Story Speaker extension in Google docs.	To relate, apply and reflect on the Human-Machine Interactions.
3- PURPOSE	Session: Introduction to sustainable development goals	To understand the impact of Artificial Intelligence on Sustainable Development Goals to develop responsible citizenship.
	Recommended Activity: Go Goals Board Game	
	• Learners to answer questions on Sustainable Development Goals	
4- POSSIBILITES	Session: Theme-based research and Case Studies	To research and develop awareness of skills required for jobs of the future.
	• Learners will listen to various case-studies of inspiring start-ups, companies or communities where AI has been involved in real-life.	To imagine, examine and reflect on the skills required for the futuristic opportunities.
	• Learners will be allotted a theme around which they need to search for present AI trends and have to visualize the future of AI in and around their respective theme.	To develop effective communication and collaborative work skills
	Recommended Activity: Job Ad Creating activity	
	Learners to create a job advertisement for a firm	

describing the nature of job available and the skill-set required for it 10 years down the line. They need to figure out how AI is going to transform the nature of jobs and create the Ad accordingly.

5- AI ETHICS

Video Session: Discussing about AI Ethics

Recommended Activity: Ethics Awareness

- Students play the role of major stakeholders and they have to decide what is ethical and what is not for a given scenario.

Session: AI Bias and AI Access

- Discussing about the possible bias in data collection

- Discussing about the implications of AI technology

Recommended Activity: Balloon Debate

- Students divide in teams of 3 and 2 teams are given same theme. One team goes in affirmation to AI for their section while the other one goes against it.

- They have to come up with their points as to why AI is beneficial and harmful for the society.

To understand and reflect on the ethical issues around AI.

To gain awareness around AI bias and AI access.

To let the students analyze the advantages and disadvantages of Artificial Intelligence.

Chapter 1
Knowledge Understanding AI

Highlights

- What is Artificial Intelligence (AI)?
- Why Artificial Intelligence?
- Pedagogy- Brainstorming/Concept maps
- Venn Diagrams
- Life Skills to be developed: Thinking Skills and Social Skills
- Inquiry and Questioning Skills
- Generating Ideas – Critical thinking skills
- Computer skills Attitude and Positive Thinking

About Artificial Intelligence:

The world 'Artificial' means made by people, not a natural or not a genuine and 'Intelligence' means the ability to understand and think. Intelligence has been defined in several ways like learning, understanding, planning, knowledge and capacity to developing logics.

Why need to be Intelligence? In the area of computer science Artificial Intelligence sometimes called Machine Intelligence and intelligence have

- Capabilities to solve the problems
- Abilities to learn
- Have a innovative plan
- To recognize patterns etc

Now Artificial Intelligence is the area of Information Technology/ computer science focusing on creating machine that can engage on behaviors that human consider intelligent. The ability to create intelligent machines has intrigued humans since ancient times and today with the advent of the computer and 60 years of research into Artificial Intelligence programming techniques and the dream of smart machines is becoming a reality..

Artificial Intelligence is a broad field and means different things to different people. It is concerned with getting computers to do tasks that require human intelligence for examples such as complex arithmetic's problems which computer can do easily. The term artificial intelligence was first coined by John McCarthy in 1956.

The main purpose of AI is to create technology that allows computer and machine to function in an intelligent manner and general problems of creating intelligence has been broken into sub- problems. There are three types of AI as

1) Weak AI

2) Strong AI

3) Super Intelligence AI

AI can be defined as "AI is a form of intelligence technique and a type of technology and a field of study". AI theory and development of computer systems (machines, computer hardware and software) are able to perform tasks that normally require human intelligence. AI is about artificial life-forms that can surpass human intelligence, and for others, almost any data processing technology can be called Artificial Intelligence.

> Our intelligence is what makes us human and AI is an extension of that quality.
>
> :- Yann LeCun

Why Artificial Intelligence?

AI is a field that overlaps with computer science rather than being a strict sub fields. Artificial intelligence, the ability of a digital computer or computer-controlled robot to perform tasks commonly associated with intelligent beings and different are of computer science. There are some different area of AI are more closely related to philosophy, psychology, linguistics and even neurophysiology healthcare, agriculture. Artificial Intelligence applications are found in many different industries from online marketing to financial services. The primary goal of AI includes knowledge representations, natural language processing, planning, learning etc.

There is some programming language which is used in development of AI projects such as:

- 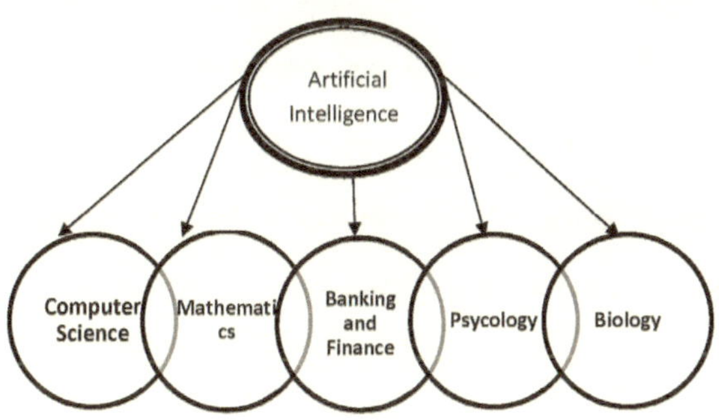 **Python:**

Python is an interpreted, object oriented, high level programming language developed by Guido van Rossum in year 1991. It is easy to read and simple to implement. It is open source means free to use even commercial application development also.

- **R Programming:**

R is a programming language which is developed in year august 1993 by Robert Gentleman and Ross Ihaka. It is a language and free software environment for graphics and statistical computing. It have graphical user interface (GUI) as a R studio which works on integrated development environment.

- **Java Programming:**

In year 1991 Java developed by Sun Microsystems. It is general purpose, object oriented, high level programming language. It is platform independent, simple familiar, distributed, secure, dynamic, high performance easy to development programming language.

These are the programming language used several area for developing artificial intelligence projects and easy to implements. For Ex.

Fig. 1.1

AI Techniques and Learning Experience form Artificial Intelligence:

AI Techniques is an organized way and methods to use the knowledge and can easily modified to correct errors or useful in may circumstances.It is a model made from advanced form for mathematical concepts. There are some examples of AI where companies adopting AI as

- Siri
- Amazon Alexa, Amazon Echo
- Spam Filters
- AI Robotics etc.

There is some core essential learning experiences area where AI techniques are post implemented:

- Creating by Identifying Problem solving
- Informed decision making
- Demonstrating responsible citizenship
- Self-reflection,
- Values
- Ethics
- exploring future career opportunities

Fig. 1.2 Example's Robot AI

Developing Proficiency for Lifelong learning:

There is some development proficiency for lifelong learning are:
- Study
- Problem solving
- Communications
- Developing Interactions
- Developing Cooperation
- Social responsibilities and applications

Fig. 1.3 Developing Proficiency Skills

Pedagogy:

In the area of an education fields, there are a few AI challenges, To use AI in a pedagogical and meaningful way, teachers need to learn new digital skills, and AI developers need to learn how teachers work and create sustainable solutions in real-life environments. AI will also work to identify weaknesses in the classroom communication problems by using ICT technology and a teacher may also be gained as a new knowledge by using technology by purely logical means through an analysis of the history of culture.

Brainstorming:

The main Purpose Brainstorming is a way to generate ideas within a group setting. It is usually used in the beginning stages of a project, where the possibilities for the project are not clearly understood or defined It provides a quick means for tapping the creativity of a limited number of people for a large number of ideas.

There are four rules of brainstorming as well as

1. No judgments
2. Think freely. As I said before, no matter how crazy it is; while brainstorming, ideas are neither silly nor impossible. ...
3. Big numbers. The more ideas, the better
4. Many heads are better than one.

<h2 style="text-align:center">Concepts of Map:</h2>

A concept of maps typically represents an ideas and information as boxes or circles which it connected with labeled arrows in downward – branching hierarchical structures.

<h2 style="text-align:center">Venn diagram:</h2>

A Venn diagram is a diagram that shows all possible logical relations between finite collections of different sets. These diagrams depict elements as points in the plane, and sets as regions inside closed curves. A Venn diagram consists of multiple overlapping closed curves, usually circles, each representing a set.

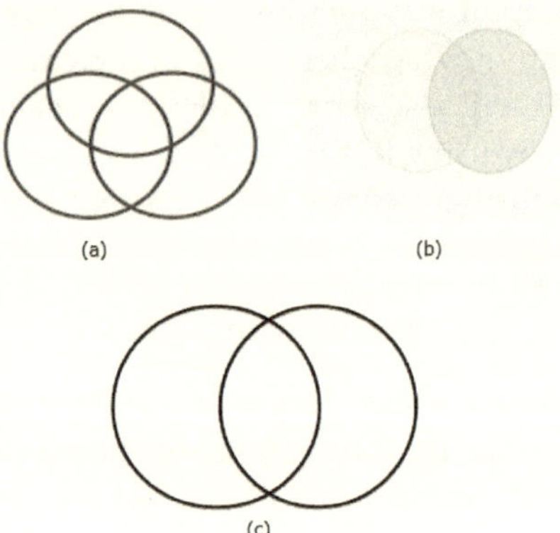

Fig. 1.4 Venn diagram

<h3 style="text-align:center">Life Skills development: Thinking Skills and Social Skills:</h3>

In the age of artificial intelligence the skills that we have to need in order to be able to think critically are varied and which includes observations, feasible study and requirements about projects and analysis.

<h3 style="text-align:center">Thinking Skills:</h3>

Thinking skills are the mental activities. We use to process information, make decisions, establishment of connections and create a new idea. There are several areas where we apply the concept of thinking skills as

- To solve the problems
- To make a plan
- To make a decision
- To ask a questions
- To organize the information

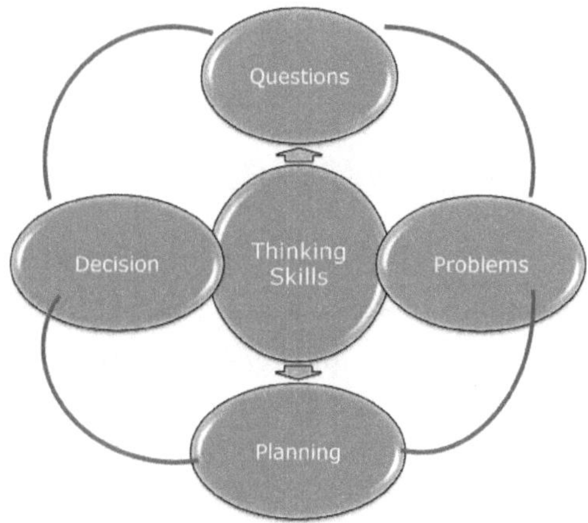

Fig. 1.5 Thinking Skill

Social Skills:

Social skill is any capability, interaction and communication with others where social rules and relations are created and changed in verbal and nonverbal way. The ability to communicate effectively with others is a core part of social skills. There are some examples of social skills as

- Active listening
- Empathy
- Relationship management
- Respect
- Flexibility
- Positive thinking
- Use proper body language
- Maintain eye contacts

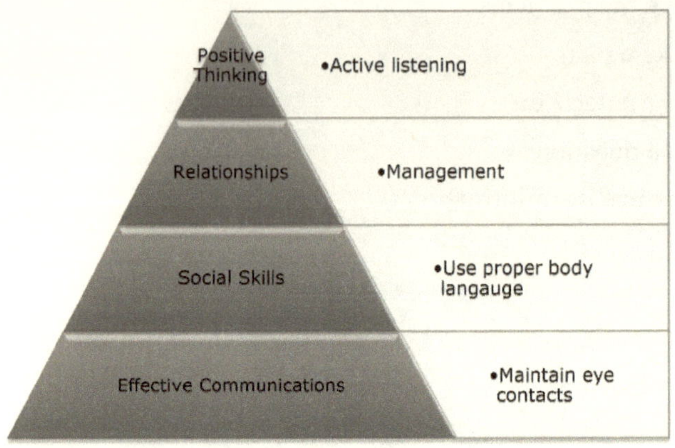

Fig. 1.6 Social Skill

Computer Skills: Attitude and Positive Thinking:

Computer skills are the ability to utilize computers and technology efficiently. It is knowledge of related technology and also in computer technology software skills involves using programs such as Microsoft office and hardware refers to the physical devices that need operating. There are some common computer skills required as

- Microsoft office
- Spreadsheets
- Email communications
- Graphics design
- Web and Social media
- Marketing automations
- Information sharing

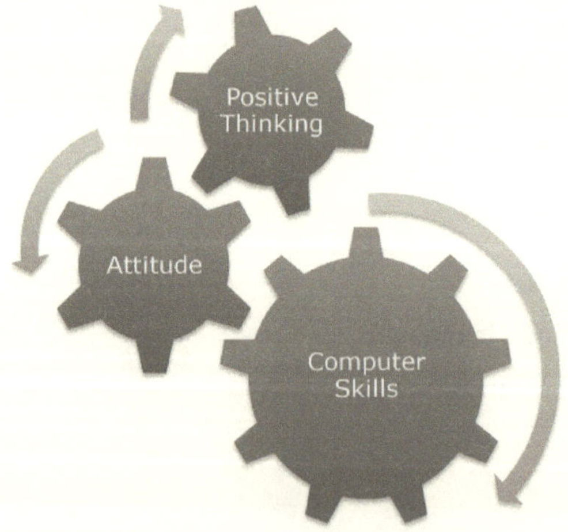

Fig. 1.7 Computer Skill

Attitude:

An attitude means the way that you think or feel or behave. Attitude is a psychological to draw, a mental and emotional entity that characterizes a person. One's attitudes reflects how one thinks, feel, and behave a given situation. Our attitude towards people, place, things or situations determines the choice that we make. It can include up to three components:

1) Behavioral

2) Cognitive

3) Emotional

Positive thinking:

Positive thinking is a mental attitude in which we expect good and favorable results. In other words we can say that positive thinking is the process of creating thoughts that create and transform energy into reality. For example when we create a project or development of software programs positive thinking is about much more than just being happy or displaying an upbeat attitude.

Critical Thinking:

In generating some idea critical thinking is the analysis of facts. It is the key of interpretations, explanations, open mindedness and problem solving. There is some area where a critical thing arises:

- Analysis

- Evaluation

- Observation

- Reflection

- Explanation

- Problem solving

- Decision making

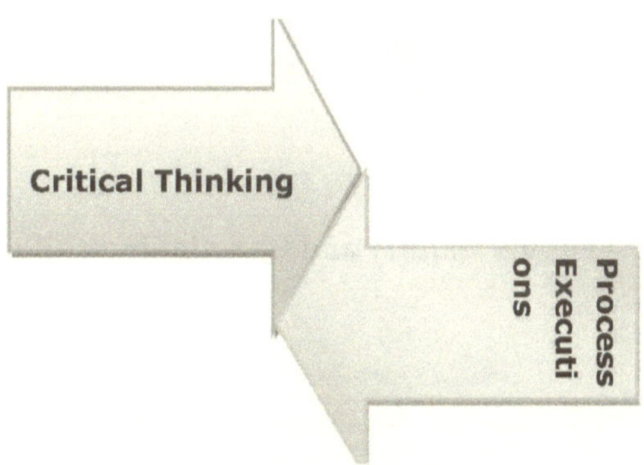

Fig. 1.8 Critical Thinking

Now we can define inquiry and questioning skills either field of educations or real words inquiry and questioning skills support investigation about technologies, area of science, mathematics or anywhere to ask the questions and analyze the potential answer. Questioning is fundamental to successful communication- we all ask and is asked questions when engaged in conversation. There are some forms of inquiry as

- Structure inquiry
- Open inquiry
- Guide inquiry
- Confirmation of inquiry

There are some steps to ask the questions as

- Decide on goal
- Select the contents for questioning
- Ask questions

For example In classroom students ask the text dependent question to their teacher that sets a expressed briefly and clearly purpose for instruction.

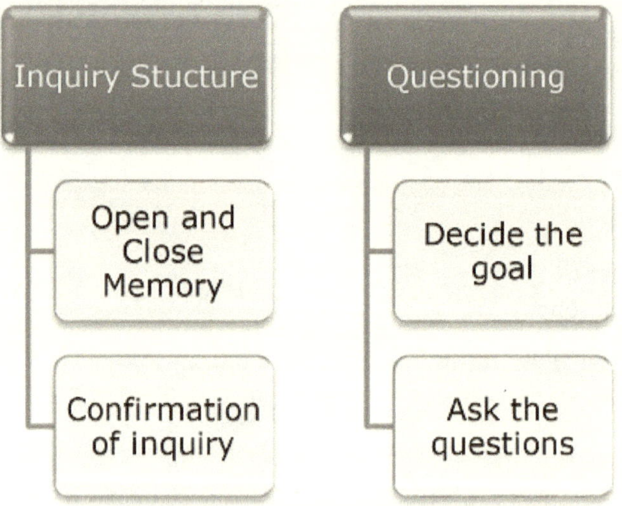

Fig. 1.9 Inquiry and Questioning skills

Exercise

A. Fill in the blanks:

1. AI is a broad field and means_ ______________people.

2. Thinking skills are the ____________________ activities.

3. The ___________effectively with other is a ________________ a social skills.

4. Positive thinking is a ________________in which we expect good and ___________________results.

B. Multiple Choice Questions:

1. There is some questioning skills have a steps.

    (a) Decide on goals

    (b) Ask questions

    (c) both a and b

    (d) None of these

2. In spreadsheets calculation, can we apply?

    (a) Artificial Intelligence

    (b) Normal Calculation formulas

    (c) both a and b options

    (d) None of these

3. ML is

    (a) Machine learning

    (b) Management learning

    (c) Microsoft language

    (d) Marquee linking

4. In brainstorming rules have.

    (a) No judgment

    (b) Judgment possible

    (c) both a and b options

    (d) None of these

C. Answer the following:

1. What is AI?
2. Why AI usable?
3. What do you understand about computer skills?
4. What id positive thinking?
5. What is critical thinking?
6. Explain the social skill briefly with diagrams.
7. Define Venn diagram.
8. What is pedagogy?
9. Define brainstorming.

Chapter 2
Unit 1- Excite

Highlights

- Introduction to Artificial Intelligence
- The relation and application of AI in our daily life
- Introduction to all three domains of AI : Data, CV,NLP
- Through Creative games using Skills based problem solving challenges
- Using all three domains in different challenging games to identify
- AI in different context

Introduction to Artificial Intelligence

About Artificial Intelligence:

In this section, we'll become familiar with the concept of AI by looking into its definition and some examples.

Artificial Intelligence has always been a term which intrigues people all over the world. Various organizations have defined their own versions of definitions of Artificial Intelligence.

"AI is about artificial life-forms that can surpass human intelligence, and for others, almost any data processing technology can be called AI".

As you have probably noticed, AI is currently a "hot topic": media coverage and public discussion about AI is almost impossible to avoid. However, we may also have noticed that AI means different things to different people. For some, AI is about artificial life-forms that can surpass human intelligence, and for others, almost any data processing technology can be called AI.

For example: Image and video processing:

Face recognition is already a commodity used in many customer, business, and government applications such as organizing your photos according to people, automatic tagging on social media like Facebook , Instagram, Pinterest etc and passport control. Similar techniques can be used to recognize other cars and obstacles around an autonomous car, or to estimate wildlife populations.

Fig. 2.1 Image processing and scanning

Self-driving cars:

Self-driving cars require a combination of AI techniques of many kinds: search and planning to find the most convenient route from Source to Destination, computer vision to identify obstacles, and decision making under uncertainty to cope with the complex and dynamic environment. Each of these must work with almost flawless precision in order to avoid accidents. The same technologies are also used in other autonomous systems such as flying drones, robots etc.

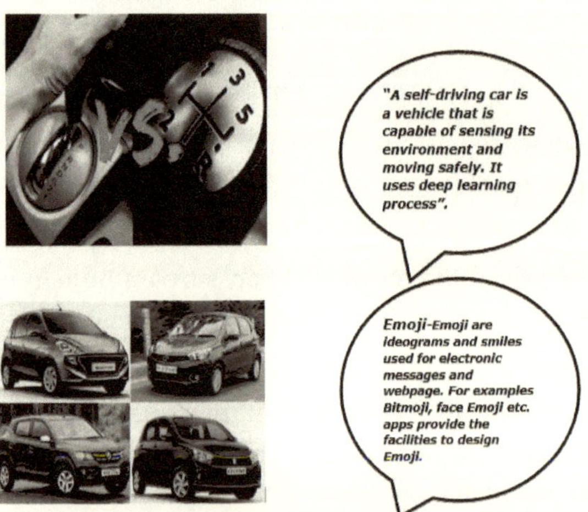

Fig. 2.2 Self driving cars and auto gears

The Relation and Application of AI in their daily life:

AI is the field of technology and science and technology based on discipline such as information technology, engineering etc. Main goal of AI is to develop computers that can think, see, hear, walk, talk and feel.

According to Rich (1987), "Artificial Intelligence is a field of study that designs and develops machines capable of performing task that would require intelligence if performed by a human being".

The application of AI can be grouped under the three major categories in our daily life:

i.   Cognitive science

ii. Robotics

iii. Natural Interface

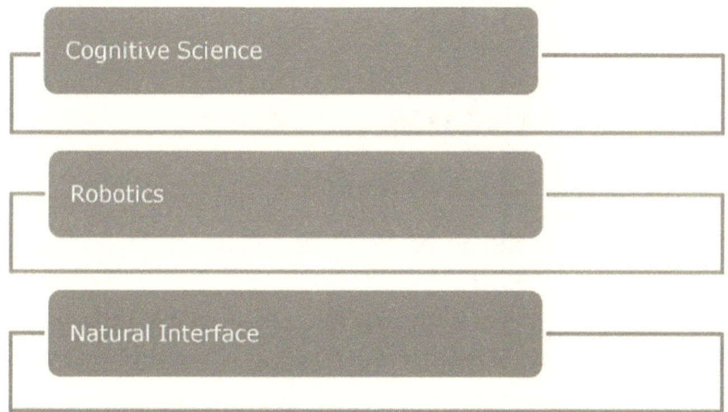

Fig. 2.3 Application of AI in our Daily life

Cognitive Science:

It is based on research in neurology, mathematics, biology, psychology, and many other disciplines. Various computer based applications in AI are developed on the basis of human information processing (HIP means how human think, learn, and how human brain works).It also includes the development of Expert system and Knowledge- based system.

Expert System:

An expert system is a software system that attempts to reproduce the performance of one or more human experts. An expert systems are designed and created to facilitate task in the field of medicine, accounting, financial services, production, and process control.

Knowledge-based System:

Knowledge based systems are represent techniques such as frames, rules, and semantic networks (SN may be used to represent knowledge.) which have originated from theory of human information processing. For examples the rules in the knowledge based are usually coded in the form: IF condition THEN action.

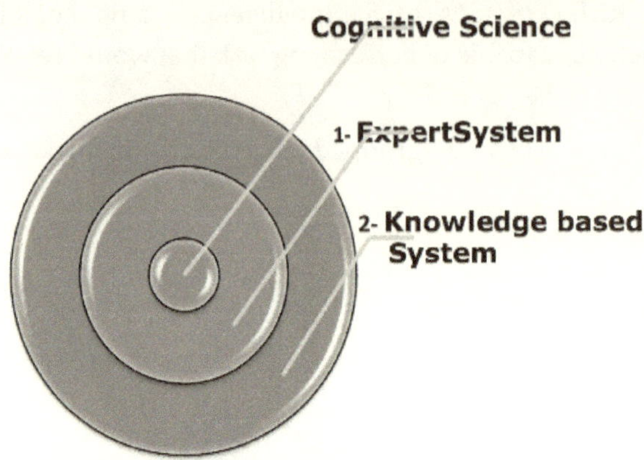

Fig 2.4 Cognitive science

Robotics:

Robotics is the science and technology of robots, their design, manufacture, and application. Robotics requires a working knowledge of electronics, mechanics and software. Robot machines has human like physical capabilities with computer intelligence and computer control. Application of Robotics provides visual perception to robot s, touch tactile capabilities, skill in handling, manipulation etc.

Natural Interface:

Natural interface is a major application area of Artificial Intelligence and it is necessary to the natural use of computers by human. For examples like speech recognition, natural languages and virtual reality (for ex. Track your body movements, tracking headset etc.)

Three domains of AI:

There are many domains and very vast area of AI. Some domains are

i.   Data for AI

ii. Natural Language Processing.(NLP)

iii. Computer Vision (CV)

iv. Voice Recognition (VR)

Data for AI:

Data we can say that a raw facts or information is all around us. The Internet of Things (IoT) and sensors have the ability to hardness large volumes of data, while artificial intelligence (AI) can learn patterns in the data or information to automate tasks for varieties of beneficial areas. AI and machine learning (ML) are going to have huge impact on manufacturing. With these technology manufacturers will gain the computational power needed to solve problems that humans can't possibly solve.

Natural Language Processing (NLP):

Natural Language Processing (NLP) refers to AI method of communicating with an intelligent system using a natural language such as English standard. Processing of Natural Language is required when we want an intelligent system like robot to perform as per your instructions, when we want to hear decision from a dialogue based clinical expert system, etc.

The field of NLP involves making computers to perform useful tasks with the natural languages humans use. The input and output of an NLP system can be –

- Speech
- Written Text

Components of NLP:

There are two components of NLP as given.

1) Natural Language Understanding (NLU)

2) Natural Language Generation (NLG)

Natural Language Understanding (NLU):

The NLU involves the following task as well as

- Mapping the given input in natural language into useful representations.
- Analyzing different aspects of the language

Natural Language Generation (NLG) :

The NLG involves the following task as

- Text planning – It includes retrieving the relevant content from knowledge base.

- Sentence planning – It includes choosing required words, forming meaningful phrases, setting tone of the sentence.

- Text Realization – It is mapping sentence plan into sentence structure.

Some Terminology Uses in Natural Language Processing:

These technical terms means nomenclature are:

- Phonology – It is study of organizing sound systematically.

- Morphology – It is a study of construction of words from primitive meaningful units.

- Morpheme – It is primitive unit of meaning in a language.

- Syntax – It refers to arranging words to make a sentence. It also involves determining the structural role of words in the sentence and in phrases.

- Semantics – It is concerned with the meaning of words and how to combine words into meaningful phrases and sentences.

- Pragmatics – It deals with using and understanding sentences in different situations and how the interpretation of the sentence is affected.

- Discourse – It deals with how the immediately preceding sentence can affect the interpretation of the next sentence.

- World Knowledge – It includes the general knowledge about the world.

Computer Vision (CV):

Computer vision (CV) is the ability to make sense of what we see, and sensing the environment. For example:

Autonomous cars apply a wide range of techniques to function and these include statistics, robotics, and machine learning and also we can understand by another example like In order to optimize ads online, machine learning and statistics are needed to deliver the correct type of ads to the right audience, and to measure the effectiveness of the optimization.

Problem 1- Let's we understand the AI from the following questions. Please read all the problems carefully and answer both of the items

1) "In GPS navigation system, can we apply AI?

2) autonomous and adaptive systems

Solution:

1) Ans. "To find out the rout we can apply the AI in GPS systems"

2) Ans. "Autonomous and adaptive systems" it highlights two main characteristics of AI, captures things like robots, self-driving cars, and so on, also nicely fits machine learning -based AI methods that adapt to the training data.

Creative games:

AI based game playing programs combine intelligence with entertainment. It is an integral part of our culture. People across the world participate in different kinds of games as a form of social interaction, competition and enjoyment.

Problem 2- Write down three rules in the given spaces you would set before playing any games?

I.

ii

iii.

Skills based Problem Solving Challenges:

For Example- Customers who bought similar products

In this problem, we will simply find out for any user, for an online shopping process where the users' purchase history is recorded and used to forecast which products the user is likely to buy next.

We have data from **six users**. For each user, we have recorded their recent shopping history of four items and the item they bought after buying these four items:

User	Shopping History				Purchase
A	Android TV	Books	Smartphone	Nokia Phone	Coffee
B	Smart watch	Coffee	coffee maker	Coffee	Coffee
C	Nokia Phone	sneakers	Smart watch	sneakers	Shoes
D	DVD Player	Smartphone	Smart watch	Android TV	Cameras
E	Smart watch	Cameras	Nokia Phone	Books	Hair Color Cream
F	Books	Coffee	DVD Player	Smartphone	Coffee

The most recent purchase is the one in the rightmost column, so for example, after buying a Smart watch, Cameras, Nokia Phone, and Books, E bought Hair Color Cream. Our hypothesis is that after buying similar items, other users are also likely to buy Hair Color Cream.

To apply the nearest neighbor method, we need to define what we mean by nearest. This can be done in many different ways, some of which work better than others. Let's use the shopping history to define the similarity ("nearness") by counting how many of the items have been purchased by both users.

For example, users E and D have both bought a Smart watch, so their similarity is 1. Note that Cameras don't count because we don't include the most recent purchase when calculating the similarity — it is reserved for another purpose.

Our task is to predict the next purchase of customer XY who has bought the following products:

User	Shopping History				Purchase
XY	green tea	Smart watch	Nokia Phone	Cameras	?

You can think of XY being our test data, and the above six users make our training data.

Proceed as follows:

Calculate the similarity of XY relative to the six users in the training data (done by adding together the number of similar purchases by the users).

Having calculated the similarities, identify the user who is most similar to XY by selecting the largest of the calculated similarities.

Predict what XY is likely purchase next by looking at the most recent purchase (the rightmost column in the table) of the most similar user from the previous step.

Que 1- Who is the user most similar to XY?

Answer: E

Correct. When you calculate the similarities between XY and all the other users, E and XY will have the largest similarity with a similarity of 3.

Que 2- What is the predicted purchase for XY?

Answer: Hair Color Cream

Correct. Since E's latest purchase was Hair Color Cream, we will recommend it also to XY.

AI in Context languages:

Context is the rules for describing block structure in programming language. It is easy to visualize in derivations and we can represent derivations using tree structure. It is applied in parser design.

Parsing:

Parsing is the process of splitting a sentence into words. There are two types of parsing like

i. Top-down parsing

ii. Bottom—up parsing

Now AI can be implemented in different context rules and algorithms but we consider only the following simple methods.

Let us see them by using context grammars rules in detail –

It is the grammar that consists rules with a single symbol on the left-hand side of the rewrite rules. Let us create grammar to parse a sentence –

Example 1- "The bird pecks the grains"

Articles (DET) – a | an | the

Nouns – bird | birds | grain | grains

Noun Phrase (NP) – Article + Noun | Article + Adjective + Noun

= DET N | DET ADJ N

Verbs – pecks | pecking | pecked

Verb Phrase (VP) – NP V | V NP

Adjectives (ADJ) – beautiful | small | chirping

The parse tree breaks down the sentence into structured parts so that the computer can easily understand and process it. In order for the parsing algorithm to construct this parse tree, a set of rewrite rules, which describe what tree structures are legal, need to be constructed.

These rules say that a certain symbol may be expanded in the form of tree by a sequence of symbols.

According to first order logic rule, if there are two strings Noun Phrase (NP) and Verb Phrase (VP), then the string combined by NP followed by VP is a sentence. The rewrite rules for the sentence are as follows –

S → NP VP

NP → DET N | DET ADJ N

VP → V NP

Lexicon –

DET → a | the

ADJ → beautiful | perching

N → bird | birds | grain | grains

V → peck | pecks | pecking

The parse tree can be created as shown-

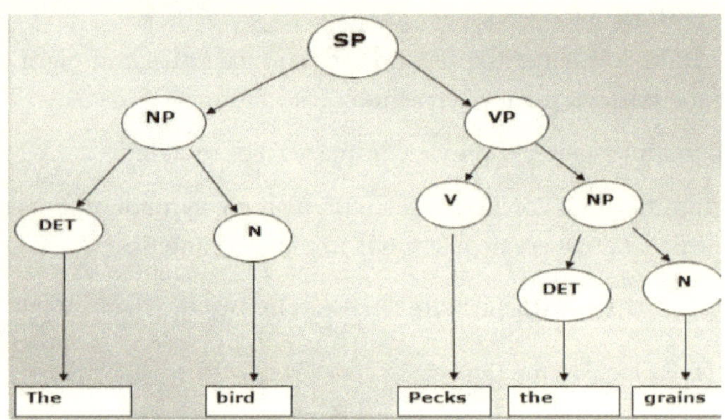

Fig. 2.5 Parsing Tree

Example 2- "Kavya ate a mango".

Now Sentence (S), Noun predicates (NP), Verb predicate (VP), Noun (N), Verb (V), and Article can be denoting as ART.

Then the Top down parsing can be as follows:

(Sentence) S ---→ NP VP (Kavya ate a mango)

     ----→ Name VP

     ----→ Kavya VN P

     ----→ Kavya ate ART N

----→ Kavya ate a N

----→ Kavya ate a mango

The Bottom-up parsing of the same sentence:

"Kavya ate a mango ---- Name ate a mango

      -----→ Name verb a mango

      -----→ Name V ART N

      -----→ NP VN P

      -----→ NP VP

      ----→ S

Activity session:

Que 1- Here are some visuals activity performs by two players in this games and you are going to play, now you have 10 seconds to guess and write the name of the games below in fig. 2.6 (a) and (b).

Fig. 2.6(a)

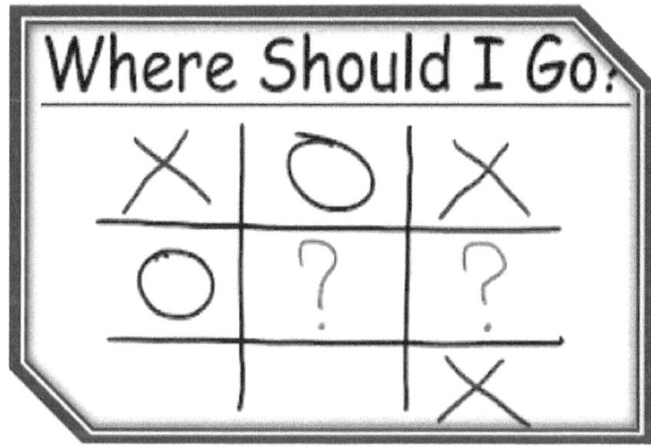

Fig. 2.6(b)

Team up with a partner and let the challenge begin!

Game 1: Rock, Paper and Scissors (based on Data)

Write three things you learnt from the game?

Ans.____

Que 2- Imagine the world in year 2030 and Write a letter to our future self. Be sure to mention things that what we think about our future self and would probably be doing and experiencing in our daily life by using figure 2.7

Some Key Terms Use in write a letter.

Date____

Place____

Area____

Benefits of AI_______________________________________

Struggle areas______________________________________

What changed_______________________________________

Fig. 2.7

Que 3- What is use of Emoji? Write the steps the following what these Emoji express.

a) ____

b) ____

c) ____

d) ____

Exercise

A. Fill in the blanks:

1. AI is currently a "hot______" media, coverage and public discussion.

2. A self driving car is _____________ that capable of sensing its environments.

3. Emoji are _______________and ___________ used for electronic___________________________.

4. _______________ based systems are represents techniques.

5. ____________ Machines has human like_________________ capabilities with computer intelligence.

6. NLP stand for____.

7. CV stands for____.

B. Multiple Choice Questions:

1. Face recognition is used for.

    (a) Programming

    (b) Security

    (c) Development

    (d) Problem solving

2. A self driving car is the example of.

    (a) Electrical engineering

    (b) Production and Transportation

    (c) AI Techniques

    (d) None of these

3. HIP means

    (a) How human think

    (b) How human learn

    (c) How human brain work

    (d) All of these

4. The input and output are an NLP system can be

   (a) Speech and written text

   (b) Special task

   (c) both a and b options

   (d) None of these

5. Context is the rules for ________________ in programming language.

   (a) Describing block structure

   (b) Describing software programs

   (c) Used in XML

   (d) Used in computing

C. Answer the Following:

1. What is AI?

2. Why we have to need AI?

3. What do you understand about image and video processing? How to scan any image?

4. What is Robotics?

5. Is AI possible in automatic self driving cars?

6. What do you understand about creative games by using AI?

7. Define computer visions (CV).

8. What is natural language processing (NLP)? What are the components of NLP?

9. Define AI in context?

10. Draw the parse tree diagram by using any examples?

Chapter 3
Unit 2- Relate

Highlights

- Learners will be able to relate to the relevance and application of AI in the context of their homes

- Learners will be able to extend learning and apply it to interactive story writing

- Human- Machine interactions

- Biotechnology

- IoT (Internet of Things)

- Alexa, Drone

- Real time Communication

Human and Machine interactions:

People might want to automate human intelligence for a number of different reasons. One reason is simply to understand human intelligence better, For example we may be able to test and refine psychological and linguistic theories by writing programs, which attempts to simulate aspects of human behavior. Another reason is simply so that we have smarter programs. We may not care if the programs accurately simulate human reasoning, but by studying human reasoning we may develop useful techniques for solving difficult problems.

"Machine learning can be said to be a subfield of AI", which itself is a subfield of computer science (such categories are often somewhat imprecise and some parts of machine learning could be equally well or better belong to statistics). Machine learning enables AI solutions that are adaptive.

So we can say that "Systems that improve their performance in a given task with more and more experience or data is called machine learning".

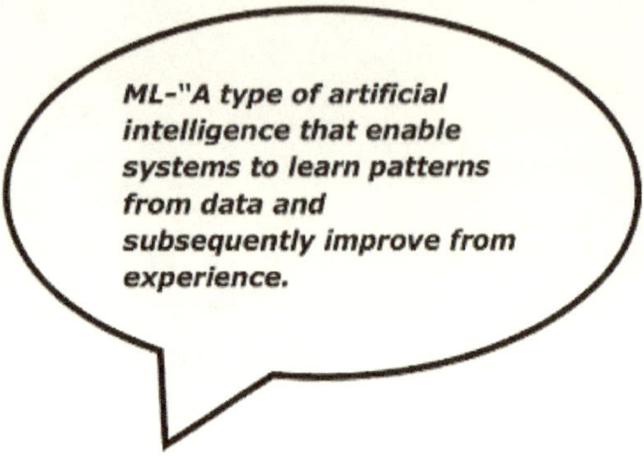

Problem 1 - What do you understand by Ice breaker activities?

Solution-

Purpose of Icebreakers:

Ice breaker games that won't make participants feel like they are wasting their time and why should you try?

The benefits of icebreakers far outweigh (to have more influence) any negatives. They can take care of introductions in a much more fun way than just simply going around the room and stating what's on your business card. They can make people remember names easier & help start conversations. When done right, icebreakers can quickly build a sense of community, set the tone for the upcoming session & give participants ownership of the learning ahead. They are also a great way for people to share their expectations, and for facilitators to introduce the topic of the day through the game. It helps participants to loosen up, understand each other more and enable better collaboration and networking.

Problem 2- For Example Name Games:

Use this ice breaker activity at, or very near, the start of a course, workshop or meeting where people don't know each other to help get to know everyone's names.

"Have the group sit in a circle where everyone can see the others". The first person says their name. The next person continues, but after saying their own name, they repeat the first person's name. This continues with each person repeating one more name. To confirm once again to people towards the end that it's ok if they get stuck & encourage the others to jump in to help if anyone is lost.

Alexa- Alexa is the products of and created by Amazon. It is a virtual assistant voice- based services that allows us to play music, check emails, make a calls, check weathers update etc.

Biotechnology: It is a technology that involves the use of living organisms. It is mainly used in

- Agriculture
- Medicine
- Food science

Internet of Things (IoT):

IoT is the growing network of objects which is connected through internet and these objects can collect the information and send data or information to each other. IoT consist of four basic elements as

1) Things- Sensors, Industry devices

2) Connectivity- To the internet, to human, to each other

3) Collect Data- By user input, from environment

4) Analytics- Enables you to take action

For example if we need to establish connectivity in smart building campus four element of IoT (Internet of Things) implemented and three links to connected in smart building campus as

1) Safety

2) Security and

3) Efficiency

Drone Camera: It is remotely controlled device. Drone camera is managed by individually software controlled device work through GPS systems. There are several areas where it is applicable now days as

- Weather monitoring
- Traffic monitoring
- Search and Rescue
- Surveillance etc

Software: Software is a computer programs which is written in a programming language required for a computer to functions or to perform a specific task.

3D Printing: It is the use of printer for creating plastic objects that are 3D form a digital model of an object that the every user would like to print for ex. Design a toys.

Real Time Communication: Real time communication is known as Online communications on the web. It have a capabilities to allow number of people to conference each other. Real time communication includes:

- File Transferring
- Any Documents application sharing
- Chatting
- Audio and Video

ALP- ALP is adaptive learning program. It is a online learning educational program which change and adapts the learning materials for educational system.

Activity session for Story Writing:

Que 1- Write a story and gain an awareness of where Artificial Intelligence is applicable at our homes surrounding areas and also relevant in their lives. Practice the story writing by using some key terms: Smart Homes and Cities and what things implemented in Smart Homes, Smart School and smart Cities by using fig 3.1.

Fig. 3.1

i. How was the activity?

ii. You can write in the space and describe the following activity:

(a). The activity was

____

(b).I learnt that

____

(c). I would

____

(d).The easy part was

____

(e).The difficult part was

____

Conversing with Story Speaker:

Que 2-How you can create a story using the Google Extension of Story Speaker for Google Docs or by using Amazon Alexa by using figure 3.2.

Fig. 3.2

i. What do you understand about the way of devices respond to your questions?

ii. What kind of information do device understand?

Que 3- Identify what new things you have added to make your dream home "smart"? By using figure 3.3

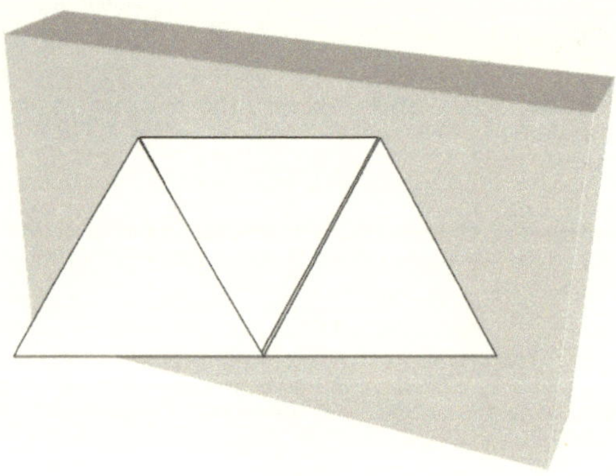

Figure 3.3

Exercise

FILL IN THE BLANKS:

1. Machine learning can be __________ to be subfield of _____.

2. The Icebreakers can quickly build a _______________ of community.

3. By studying human reasoning we may __________ useful _________________ for solving difficult_______________.

B. Multiple Choice Questions:

1. ML is a type of AI that enables systems to learn__________.

    (a) Patterns

    (b) Process

    (c) Compilations

    (d) None of these

2. To design a Smart home we can use_________________.

    (a) AI Techniques

    (b) Smart roof

    (c) Smart Color

    (d) All of these

3. Google Assistant is

    (a) Voice assistant

    (b) Only Operations

    (c) only for story writing

    (d) None of these

4. Microphone used for

    (a) Voice recording

    (b) Display movie

    (c) For Connectivity

    (d) None of these

5. Alexa is the products of

(a) Apple

(b) Microsoft

(c) Amazon

(d) Dell

6. Skype use for

(a) Online communication

(b) Offline communication

(c) both a and b options

(d) None of these

7. in smart school we can use

(a) Digital smart board

(b) Smart computers

(c) Android based H/W and S/W devices

(d) All of these

C. Answer the following:

1. What do you think Artificial Intelligence is?

2. What will you learn about use of Amazon Alexa or "Echo"?

3. Write a plan how to create a smart floor at your home. Draw the diagrams?

4. Define ML.

5. What is the use of Amazon echo?

6. How is Google assistant work?

7. How we can connect our smart phone with android devices?

8. Define biotechnology.

9. What do you understand by IoT?

Chapter 4
Unit- 3- Purpose

Highlights

- Learners will be able to identify and develop awareness
- What is SD?
- Introduction to 17 sustainable development goals(SDG)
- About Sense
- Use of Waze

Develop awareness in the field of AI:

AI is the branch of computer science and engineering that emphasizes the development of an intelligence machine, learning, planning, and also speech recognition.

"According to NITI Aayog-

NITI Aayog has decided to focus five sectors of AI to solving societal needs as well as

1. Agriculture
2. Healthcare
3. Education
4. Smart cities
5. Transportations"

Type of AI:

1. Theory of Mind
2. Limited memory
3. Self-awareness

Advantages of Artificial Intelligence:

- Digital Assistance
- Handling routine tasks as 24*7 Available
- Finding mistakes of human
- Fast in Decision making
- Handling area of research and medical diagnosis
- Solve the Complex Problems
- Used in Daily Applications like Google 'Ok' etc

What is sustainable development?

Sustainable Development is development that meets the needs of the present without compromising the ability of future generations to meet their own needs as well.

Sustainable development requires simultaneous and balanced progress in three dimensions that are totally depending on each other. There are four dimensions of sustainable development process as

1) Sustainability

2) Society

3) Economics and

4) Environments

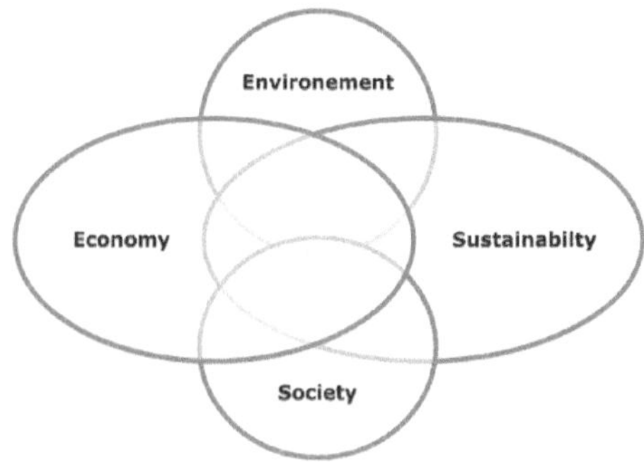

Fig. 4.1 Sustainable Development Dimensions

Sustainable Development Goals (SDG):

In sustainable development process artificial intelligence is speedly opening up a new fields which is going on Government sectors, corporate etc. The intelligence of machines and robotics with deep learning capabilities for government, societis and management education. AI can significantly affect the work of advancing SDGs. This world is the home for life of people, plants and animals. The materials and resources that the planet provides help us to sustain life. In order to build a better world for everyone it is important that we take care to conserve, preserve and protect our Shelter and the life of those in this world. The Member States of the United Nations have agreed to achieve 17 Sustainable Development Goals (SDGs) by 2030.

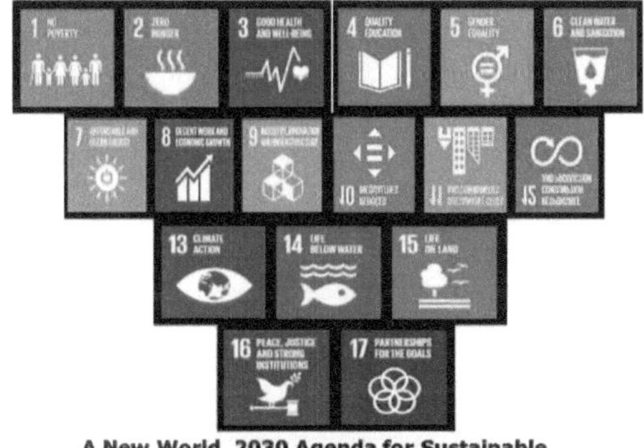

Fig 4.2 A New World Agenda of SDGs 2030

Now a days an international organisation which engage in worldwide business, political and academic agendas. For example we can describe the government technological agenda through a following daigram and also implements the what are resources need? And some higher autherization policy analyzes to achievement of sustainable development goals.

Example- Diagram of SDG

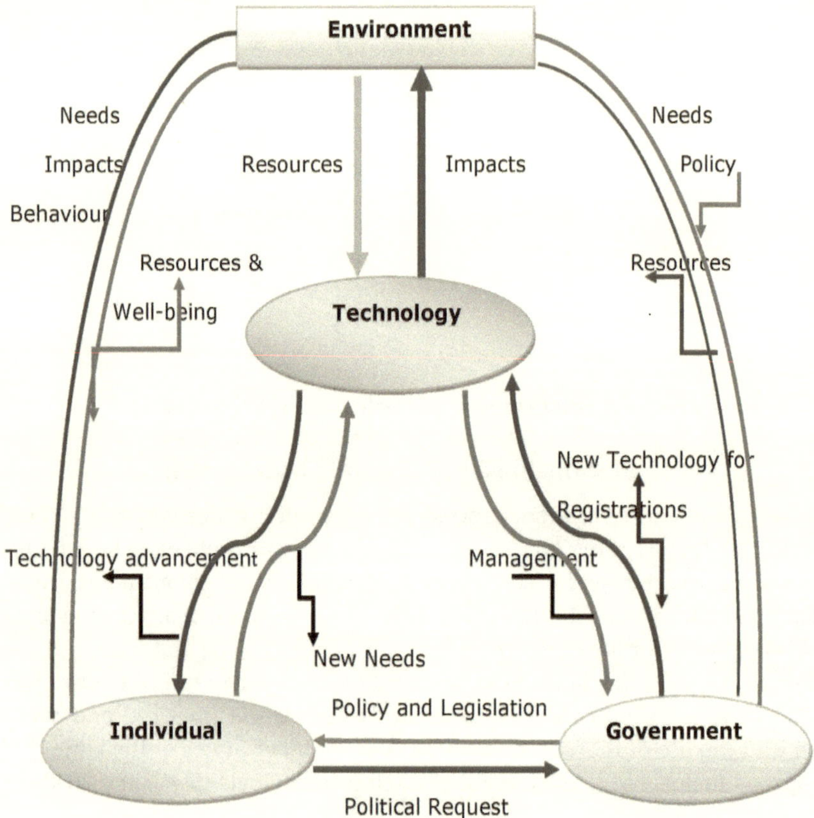

Fig. 4.3 SDG

There are the 17 sustainable development goals (SDGs) to transform our world as well as

- Quality of Education
- No Poverty
- Gender equality
- Good health
- Clean water and Sanitation
- Clear Energy
- Economics growth

- Reduce inequalities

- Zero Hunger

- Sustainable cities and communities

- Good Productions

- Peace and Justice strong institutions

- Climate action

- Industry, innovation and infrastructures

- Life below water

- Life on land

- Partnership for achieving the Goals

For example- Sustainable Achievement goals or urban and rural ares-

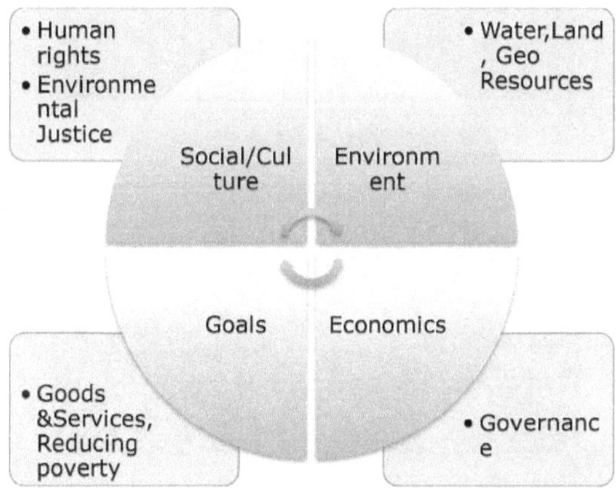

Fig. 4.4 Sustainable Achievement Goals

Activity Session:

Que 1- Are you satisfied with the things happening around you, which are shown in figure 4.5?

Fig. 4.5

Que 2- Look at the following picture 4.6 and write the actions you will take.

Fig. 4.6

Que 3- Write your own thoughts or opinion to see the following pictures 4.7 (a) and 4.7 (b).

Fig.4.7 (a)

Fig. 4.7 (b)

Que-4 By using figure number (4.5), (4.6), (4.7 a), and (4.7 b) Can we play a role in helping or supporting work in the following areas and other areas that contribute to well-being of the planet and people?

(Tick the appropriate box)   **Yes   No**

- **Removing poverty**   [ ]   [ ]
- **Clean Water**   [ ]   [ ]
- **Clean Energy**   [ ]   [ ]
- **Good Health care**   [ ]   [ ]
- **Preventing Hunger**   [ ]   [ ]
- **Equality of Gender**   [ ]   [ ]
- **Others (Write an Essay)**   **[Tips: Use AI Techniques]**

Exercise

A. Fill in the blanks:

1. AI is branch of _________________ science and engineering.
2. SDG expands for ______________________________________.
3. AI has a self ____.
4. NITI Aayog has decided for focus of _________________ of AI.
5. Loss of _____________________ is the disadvantage of AI.
6. Finding _________________ of human is the advantage of AI.

B. Multiple Choices of Questions:

1. AI emphasized the development of
   (a) Speech recognition
   (b) Planning
   (c) Machine learning
   (d) All of these
2. AI can significantly affect the _________ of advancing SDGs.
   (a) Work
   (b) Computer
   (c) Marketing
   (d) None of these
3. There are _______ sustainable development goals to transform our world.
   (a) 19
   (b) 17
   (c) 21
   (d) 15
4. Waze is a mapping and navigation application for mobile devices, acquired by Google in year_____________________.
   (a) 2013
   (b) 2010
   (c) 2014
   (d) 2020

5. An international organisation which engage in

    (a) Worldwide Business

    (b) Political Agenda

    (c) Academic Agenda

    (d) All of these

6. _______________ language is easy to learn and one of the most popular language for AI Today.

    (a) C#

    (b) Python

    (c) Java

    (d) Ruby

C. Answer the following:

1. What is 17 sustainable development goals (SDG)? Briefly explain with examples.

2. How we can identify the develop awareness in the field of AI?

3. What are the advantages and disadvantages of AI?

4. Draw the SDG diagrams.

5. What are the five sectors of AI to solving societal needs decided by NITI Aayog?

6. What is Waze?

Chapter 5
Unit-4- Possibilities

Highlights

- Describe and explore the application of AI in different fields and various industries.

- To develop effective communication and collaborative work skills.

- To imagine, examine and reflect on the skills required for the futuristic opportunities.

- K-R (Knowledge Representation)

- Expert System

- Deep learning

- Strong, Weak and Responsible AI

- Remote Learning

Applications of Artificial Intelligence in Different Areas:

There are two main objective of AI are: To improve the potential of computer as a tool for solving the problems and second one To improve the understanding of human. Applications of AI can be categories in three major categories like Robotics, Cognitive science and natural interface, but here we discuss some new technology and developments in commercial applications of artificial intelligence. The most practical applications of AI is knowledge based system which is used to find knowledge and provide better solutions to end users.

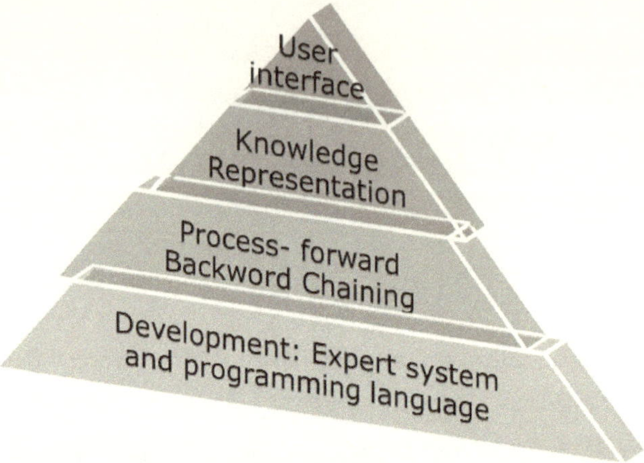

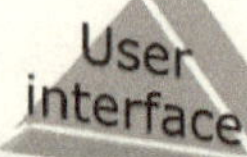

Fig. 5.1 Application of AI

There are some AI Applications as

- AI In Sale and Marketing:
    - Give response to inquiries of customers
    - To focus policies of discount
    - Establishment of sale and marketing quotas
- AI In Banking sectors:

> ***Expert System-* *It is a software system that attempts to reproduce the performance of one or more human experts. It facilitate tasks in the field of medicine, production, HR etc***

- o   Implementation of technology
- o   Online solutions
- o   Transactions and process management
- o   Good communications
- o   Provide security to customers
- o   Flexibility
- o   Reliability in operations
- AI In Finance and Commercial sectors:
  - o   Analyze customers' behaviors
  - o   Using AI assistants
  - o   Smart logistics
  - o   E-commerce company uses machine learning
  - o   Using Chatbots
  - o   Visibility in e-commerce space

- AI In Agriculture.
  - o   Understanding and Planning
  - o   Automation of firming activities
  - o   Using fertilizers
  - o   Using ML in agriculture
  - o   Using new technologies time to time

- AI In HealthCare.
  - o Implementation of advance technology
  - o AI based applications
  - o Great services
  - o Diagnosis' process treatment
  - o Drug Development
  - o Patient monitoring and care
- AI In Gaming
  - o Feasible study
  - o Analysis and requirements
  - o Create a structure
  - o Solve the complexity
  - o Uses IoT
- AI In Education
  - o Using emerging technology
  - o Virtual Networking
  - o Online solutions by using Machine learning and IoT
  - o Best way to leaning environment
  - o Voice assistants
  - o Intelligent Chatbots
  - o E-mailing
  - o Easy to communication
- AI In Autonomous Vehicles and Manufacturing

o   Selecting routes for transportation

o   Scheduling task

o   Maintaining facilities

o   Analyze quality of products

o   Determine the correction of a running process

o   Modification and implementations

To Development of Effective Communication:

AI is the area of CS and information technology that can engage on behaviour s that humans consider intelligent. The internet is very important to helps in computing and provides to development of technology in various sectors and provides a process of communication capabilities. An applications that uses internet based technologies are less expensive to develop, maintain, and operate than other traditional systems. There are various tools and areas to development of effective communications as

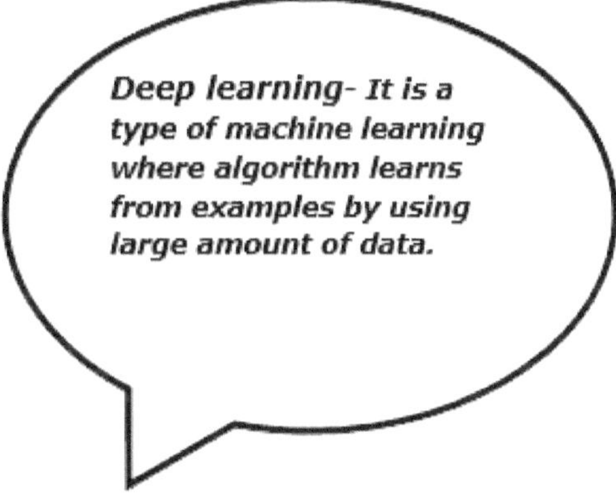

* E-mail
* Group discussion forums
* Telnets
* Online services
* To maintain a public relations
* Easy services to all internet based platforms
* Business to business and consumers
* Reduce the paper works
* Low costing
* Provide better, fast, and effective linkage with the clients

Collaborative Work Skills

Collaborative work skill helps people to accomplish or manage joint work activities. It is used to manage workgroup projects and team to take necessary action that information is collected at the right time and right place. It may be noted that information is the process data and the process information is action. It includes

- Workflow systems,
- Calendaring and
- Scheduling tools,
- Knowledge repositories,
- Task and
- Project management
- Joint document creation
- Editing and
- Revision

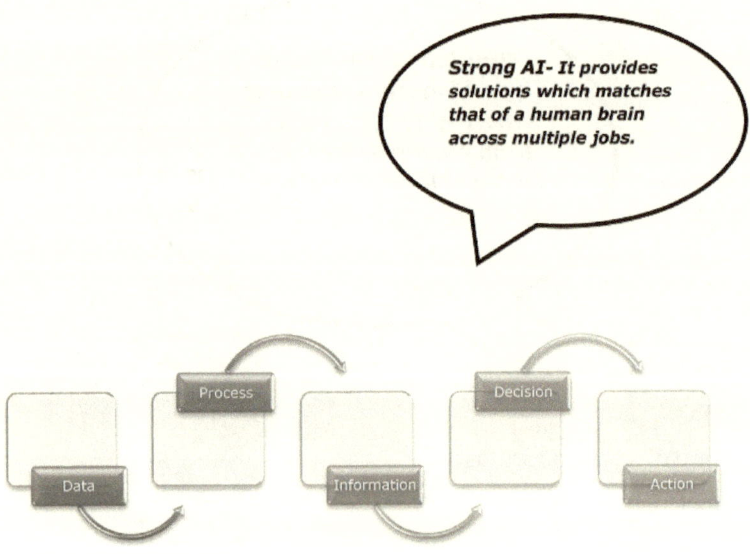

Fig. 5.2 Collaborative Work Process ()

**To Imagine, Examine and reflect on the Skills
required for the Futuristic Opportunities.**

In area of artificial intelligence an expert system is the most practical application which is knowledge base which able to explain the required skills and conclusions to a user. Futuristics are people interest to attempt to systematically predictions and possibilities about future and how we can emerge from the present to implement of machine learning and Internet of Things(IoT). There are some areas of skills as

- Problem solving
- Critical thinking
- Effective oral and Written communications
- Assessing and analyzing information
- Imaginations
- Curiosity
- Adaptability
- Collaboration of across networks
- Entrepreneurship
- Creativity
- Emotional intelligence
- Being technology savvy
- Leadership skills
- Decision making
- Diverse team management
- Transparency
- Managing the future

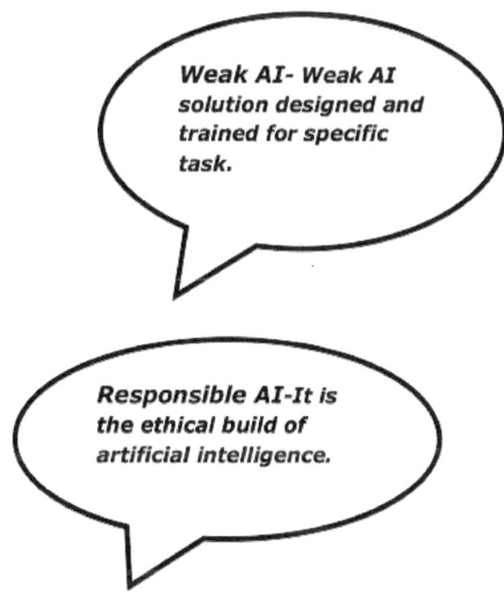

The imagination of future work skills offers an opportunities and unpatrolled work but also significant challenges. The examines solve the complex problems and ability to take challenges of changing the area of society and labour markets.

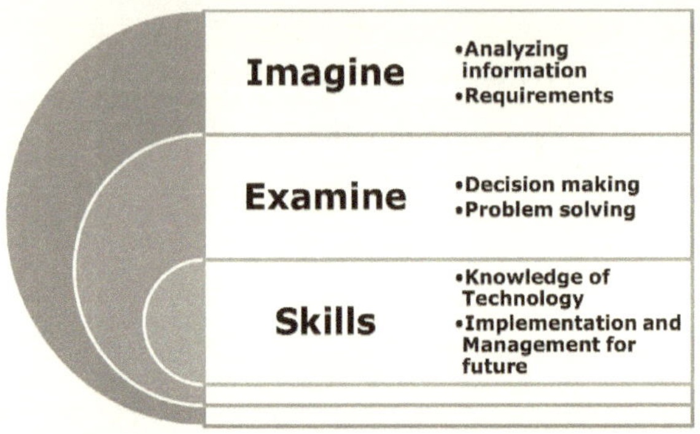

Fig. 5.3 Futuristics opportunities

Remote Learning:

It is a virtual learning or training process in which we can to take place synchronously .Remote learning is also known as distance learning to allows teachers to deliver their lessons online and student can complete their tasks just like they would be in the classroom.

Remote Work:

Remote work is online or virtual working style that allows us to work outside of traditional office environments.

Activity Session:

Que 1- Try to analyze what skill-sets would be required 10 years down the line which is shown in figure 5.4? Also, look at the skill-sets required for such jobs today.

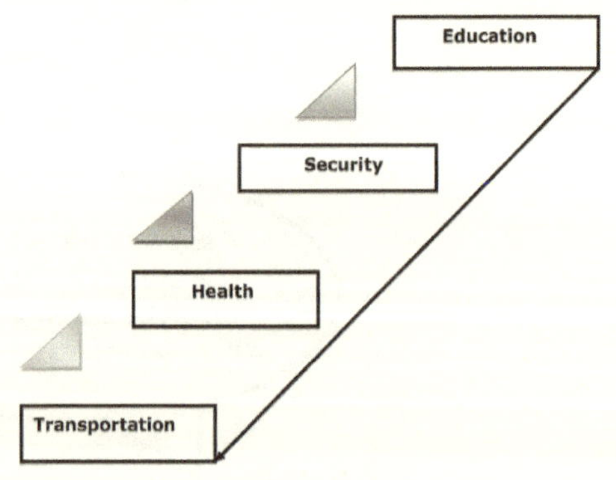

Figure 5.4

Exercise

A. Fill in the blanks:

1. Knowledge represent system solves the _____________ problems.

2. The most practical application of Artificial Intelligence is _______________ based system.

3. An application of AI can be categories in _______ major categories.

4. _________ system facilitate tasks in the ___________ of medicine, productions etc.

5. Deep learning is a type of _______________________.

6. Collaborative work skill helps people to _________ joint_______________ activities.

7. The examiner solve the ____________ problems and ability to take challenges of ________ the area of ___________ markets.

B. Multiple Choice Questions:

1. Weak AI solution designed and trained for_____________

    (a) Specific task

    (b) No task

    (c) Networking

    (d) All of these

2. PayPal is a _______________payment system.

    (a) Offline

    (b) Online

    (c) both a and b

    d) None of these

3. Intelligent voice system is a __________________.

    (a) Hardware

    (b) Software

    (c) Networking

    (d) Messenger

4. AI is autonomous vehicles and manufacturing have__________

   (a) Selecting routs

   (b) Scheduling task

   (c) Maintaining facilities

   (d) All of these

C. Answer the following:

1. Define the applications of AI in briefly.

2. What do understand about collaborative work skills?

3. What skills required implementing of AI in Futuristics opportunities?

4. What is effective communications?

5. Write the steps to use of AI in gaming.

6. What are the uses of AI in health sectors?

7. What is deep learning?

8. Define expert system.

9. Differentiate between weak AI and strong AI.

D. Define some key Terms:

1. KR

2. PayPal

3. IVS

4. Responsible AI

Chapter 6
Unite 5- Ethics

Highlights

- Learners will be able to describe some ethical concerns of AI with respect to inclusion,.

- Big data

- AI bias,

- Privacy

- Awareness to Ethics

- Advantages and disadvantages of Artificial Intelligence

Ethics of Artificial Intelligence:

The ethics of AI lies in the ethical quality of its prediction, the ethical quality of the end outcomes drawn out of that and the ethical quality of the impact it has on humans. Ethics is also defined as: The discipline dealing with right vs. wrong and the moral obligations and duties of humans.

Fig. 6.1

Some of the widely-used AI in the world that we know manifests as smart tools and virtual assistants that power technologies such as Google assistant Apple's Siri, or Amazon's Alexa. Microsoft Cortana too, has championed its own deep learning natural language processing technology. For example Replika, Snap-chat, AI based apps which also used natural language processing. AI is also used for <u>automated facial recognition</u>, or in <u>big data analytics</u>, in which data is assessed to derive insights that can drive sharper business decision-making. There are some ethics principles in AI as

- Commit and delegate
- Collect and share information
- Ideate and iterate
- Validate
- Start using
- Develop

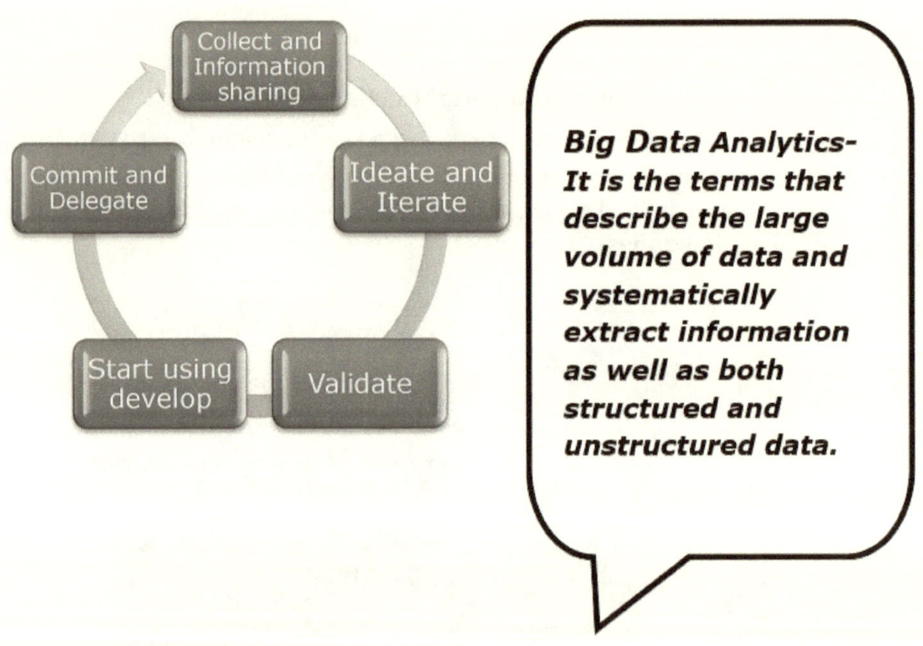

Fig. 6.2 Ethics Principle of AI

AI with Inclusion:

Artificial intelligence (AI) and inclusion mean different things to different people. An objectives of an inclusion with AI to discussion of any forums or workshops, meeting to encourage participants to develop a shared understanding of the complex concepts of AI and inclusion across disciplinary, geographic, cultural etc.

When considering the social impact of AI, conceptualizing inclusion may become even more difficult because AI systems are powered by pattern recognition and classification, which, broadly speaking, often drive exclusionary social processes. Because of this, AI has feedback effects on the notion of inclusion itself.

AI Bias:

In area of artificial intelligence Machine learning bias, also known as algorithm bias or AI bias is a phenomenon that occurs when an algorithm produces results that are systematically prejudiced due to erroneous assumptions in the machine learning process.

It means we can understand"Bias" is an overloaded term which means remarkably different things in different contexts"

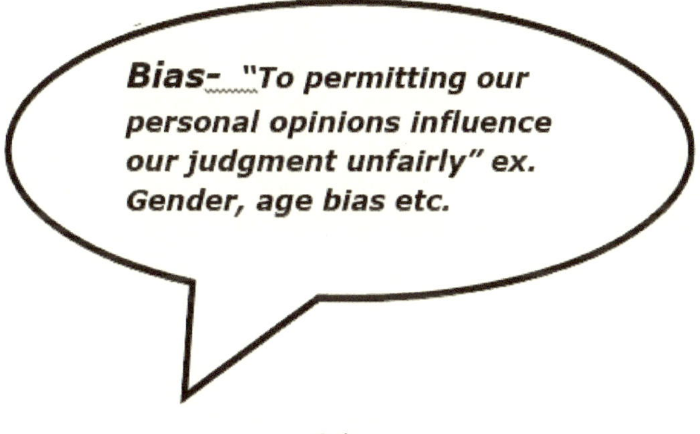

Privacy:

As artificial intelligence evolves, it magnifies the ability to use personal information in ways that can to thrust on privacy interest by raising analysis of personal information to new levels of power and speeds like "facial recognition systems".

Ethical Awareness:

Ethical awareness is the ability to identify moral or ethical issues and the inclination to do something about them. In philosophy, "ethics" has three main branches. Ethical awareness is the ability to identify moral or ethical issues and the inclination to do something about them. Ethics has three main branches as

1. Justice

2. Generosity

3. Charity

The ethical awareness may include the following:

- Identifying an ethical problem

- Assessing how serious the issue is

- Communicating this problem to others in the community

- Changing one's own perspective to see the issue from a different angle

- Predicting how an ethical issue could affect others in the workplace

Artificial Intelligence in Everyday Life:

Artificial intelligence affects our life in many programs and services that help us do everyday things such as connecting with friends, using an email program, or using a ride-share service. There are several areas as

- **E-commerce organizations-**In this organization like Flipcart, Amazon, Tata Cliq and Ali Baba use AI to understand customer purchase behavior and to subsequently make recommendations.

- **Financial Sectors-** In this sector deploy AI techniques to mine for fraudulent transactions in order to keep your data and money safe.

- **Digital assistants-**By using digital assistants like Google assistants Siri and Alexa understand our voice and questions to provide the solutions and information or to execute tasks.

- **Networking platforms-** In the area of networking like Replika, Snap chat apps use AI and Facebook also use AI to detect if there has been unauthorized access of our images. Microsoft also used IoT and AI based applications for business apps like Microsoft team apps to everyone. Some Companies make use of AI applications called Chatbots to provide customer support. These Chatbots provide wide range of services. They can resolve our queries, book appointments and provide better solutions for example Tatasky dish TV etc.

How Artificial Intelligence Improves Social Media?

Artificial intelligence makes it easier for users to locate and communicate with friends and business associates. Some of the ways you may be benefitting from AI on social media are like Twitters, Facebook, Facebook messenger, Whatsapp, Instagram, and Pinterest etc. for example Google provides the email services and have several options and facilities like:

- Primary
- Social
- Promotions
- Updates
- Forums
- Spam
- Trace

These program help our emails get organized way. Gmail sorts each email into different tabbed categories, and sends the spam mail to a spam folder.

Advantages of Artificial Intelligence:

- Digital Assistance
- Handling routine tasks as 24*7 Available
- Finding mistakes of human
- Fast in Decision making
- Handling area of research and medical diagnosis
- Solve the Complex Problems
- Used in Daily Applications like Google 'Ok' etc

Disadvantages of Artificial Intelligence:

- Loss of jobs- Loss of jobs, risk includes capturing positions etc.
- Lack of values- Like subjective judgments, empathy etc.
- No Emotions
- Making Humans Lazy

Activity Session:

Que 1- Imagine there are two families of four people out for a ride in a hot air balloon. Suddenly the balloon in figure 6.3 starts to move towards the earth instead of staying airborne. To stabilize it, one family needs to take the parachute and go out of the balloon or else it will come crashing down. Who should be thrown out of the hot air balloon?

Figure 6.3

Answer-

1. ____

2. ____

3. ____

4. ____

Que 2- Prepare the points of debate in favour of AI or against of AI around the following themes 6.4..

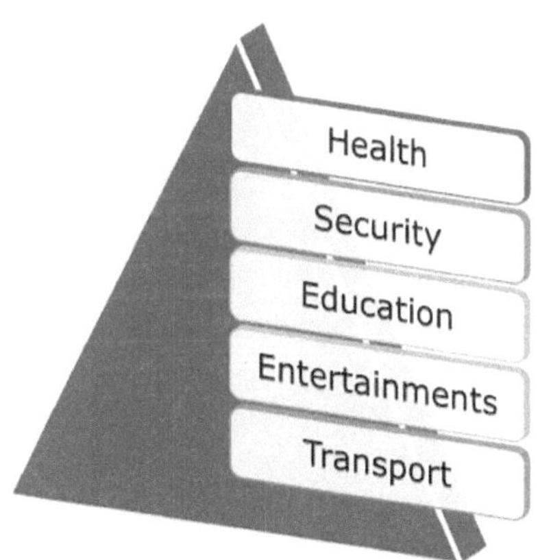

Theme 6.4

Answer.

____

____

____

____

<h1 align="center">Exercise</h1>

A. Fill in the blanks:

1. AI is also used for automated _______________ recognitions.

2. AI and Inclusion means different ___________ to _________ people.

3. Machine learning bias is also known as ___________ bias.

4. In philosophy ethics has _________ main branches.

5. Artificial Intelligence makes it easier for users to ___________ and _____________with friends and business associates.

6. In Gmail Spam folder consists_______________ messages.

B. Multiple Choice Questions:

1. Big data is the terms that describes the large volume of data as

(a) Structured Data

(b) Unstructured Data

(c) both a and b options

(d) none of these

2. To permitting our personal opinions influence our personal judgment unfairly is called

(a) R programming

(b) Security

(c) Bias

(d) Natural language

3. Ethics has___________________ branches as

(a) Justice

(b) Generosity

(c) Charity

(d) All of these

4. An example of E- Commerce company is

(a) Door to Door Business

(b) Extranet

(c) Flipcart

(d) Facebook

5. Google assistant understand the user commands for

   (a) Voice

   (b) Problems

   (c) Output

   (d) none of these

6. Chatbots used for

   (a) Offline conversations

   (b) Online conversations

   (c) both a and b options

   (d) none of these

7. In outlook mail box deleted messages store in

   (a) Group folder

   (b) Draft folder

   (c) Rubbish folder

   (d) Archive folder

C. Answer the following:

1. What do you understand about ethics of AI. Explain with diagram?

2. What is AI bias?

3. Define the term privacy.

4. How can affect AI to human in every day of life?

5. How AI improved the social media?

6. What is ethical awareness of AI?

7. What do you understand about inclusions of AI?

8. How will human beings ensure that they stay ahead of Artificial Intelligence?

9. How do you think income would be shared if Ai is used in place of Human Workforce?

10. What is big data?

11. AI is a powerful tool in various fields, however depending on how it is used, Discuss.

Project Work

Project 1:

Write an application about expressions of Emoji and to create an Electronic page to display the keywords of Emoji.

Project Descriptions:

- Use paper and pencil to draw an Emoji
- Use the Android Smartphone
- Draw the Emoji buttons for expressions
- Display the Emoji in an electronic media
- Display the final Emoji on board with their expressions

For Example: Emoji Format-

Project 2:

Write a project to create a smart home and smart cities by using some electronic media and devices to use your home and cities like cleaning your home and cities etc.

Project Descriptions:

- Access the video by using the YouTube apps or webpage.
- Using their own creativity and knowledge
- Draw the paper work
- Use the smart devices for home and cities
- Focus what equipments needed
- Use Google assistants, Amazon Alexa and Echo
- Watch the Amazon Prime Video also for smart cities
- To make a smart office at your cities
- Use room cleaner like MI –Vacuum cleaner robot for home and cities.

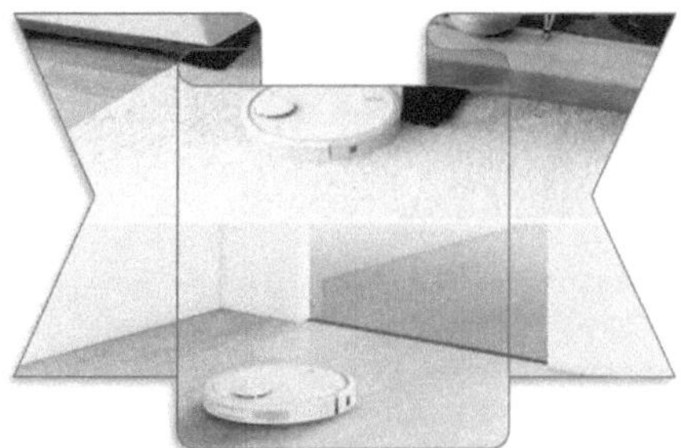

Project 3:

Draw an activity as Students divide in teams of 3 and 2 teams are given same theme. One team goes in affirmation to AI for their section while the other one goes against it. Why AI is beneficial and harmful for the society. Use some following images (a), (b), (c) and describe it.

a)

b)

c)

Project 4:

Watch the following you tube video with help of internet and create a school culture program with help of computer hardware and some devices.

Project Descriptions:

- Use Computer H/W, S/W and some devices

- Use Smartphone, Audio devices, microphone, and internet services

YouTube Link: https://youtu.be/l15dNy7Huv8

https://youtu.be/feyg2d2t3sM

Example: Channel name- Divine Techie:

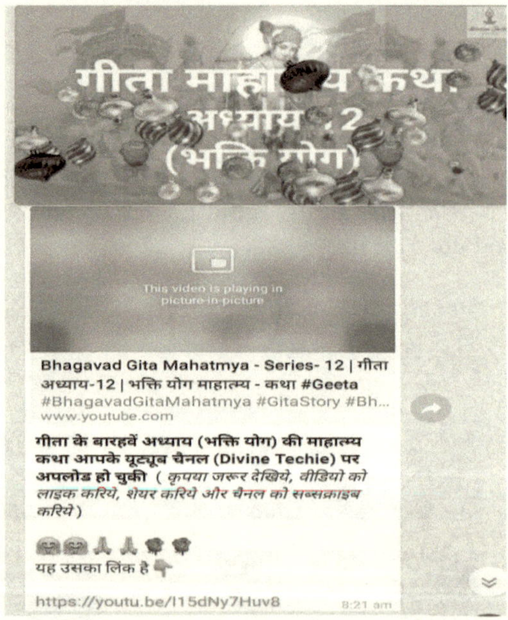

IT Terms

- Facebook Messenger- Used for online chatting, video, audio calling facilities

- Whatsapp- Online communication apps used for android applications

- Android OS- It is Linux based operating system designed for touch screen tablets and mobile phone developed by android Inc.

- Skype App- Skype have a facilities for online connectives to number of user and offered by Microsoft Company.

- Zoom App- Used for online meeting, virtual study classes etc.

- Microsoft Team - Used for online meeting, chatting and sharing messages

- Duo- This is Google duo and used for audio calling and at a time more than 10 members connect through video calling, create a group and communicate with each other.

- Replika- It is AI based application used for personal assistant and sharing information.

- Snap chat- It is AI based social application used for chatting.

- Cortana- It is voice activated personal assistant used in windows based applications and android also, offered by Microsoft.

- Robin- AI based voice assistant

- Uber- It is American based transportation company and it uses app-based system to pickup and drop facilities to passenger at desired locations.

- BIOS: Basic Input Output System

- HDD: Hard disk Drive used for storage of information

- SATA: It is Software- Defined Storage for separates the data storage from its associated software.

- VGA: It is Video Graphics Array for displaying graphics and developed by IBM.

- USB: The Universal Serial Bus is used for communications between certain devices.

- **VRML:** It is a Virtual Reality Markup Language allows displaying of 3D images.

- **VR:** It is a Virtual Reality which simulates three dimensional scenes on the computer. It is widely used in gaming.

- **BYOC:** Bring your own cloud. It is a cloud based file sharing software.

- **VDI:** It can be used for virtually desktop access by several users.

- **SaaS:** It stands for Software as a Service and work on demand software stored in cloud.

- **SSD:** It stands for Solid State Drive and more modern type of hard drive that has no moving parts.

ABBREVIATIONS

- AI : Artificial Intelligence
- ASR : Automatic Speech Recognition
- CAL : Computer Aided Learning
- CAD : Computer Aided Design
- DL : Deep Learning
- ML : Machine Language
- KR : Knowledge Representation
- RCT : Remote Class room Training
- DE : Distance Education
- DL : Distance Learning
- RL : Remote Learning
- RT : Remote Training
- VT : Virtual Training
- VL : Virtual Learning
- RW : Remote Work
- VC : Video Conferencing
- OSOC : Open Schedule Online courses
- API : Application Programming Interface
- URL : Uniform Resource Locators
- Internet : International Network
- 5G : Fifth Generation
- LCD : Liquid Crystal Display
- CASE : Computer Aided Software engineering
- ISO : International Standard Organization
- SCSI : Small Computer Scale Interface
- E-Mail : Electronic mail
- DMA : Direct Memory Access

- HTTP : Hyper Text Transfer Protocols
- WWW : World Wide Web
- C-DAC : Center for Development and advanced Computing
- FAT : File Allocation Table
- SQL : Structured Query Language
- VIOP : Voice Over Internet Protocols
- WB : Web Browser
- PDF : Portable Document Format
- PC : Personal Computer
- ISP : Internet Service Provider
- PPP : Point to Point Protocols
- SEO : Search Engine Optimization
- WYSIWYG What You See Is What You Get
- VPN : Virtual Private Network
- VDI : Virtual Desktop Infrastructure
- FKP : Facial Key Points
- GAL : Get A Life